Hillary Clinton:

Truth and Lies

I0411144

By
Max Vanguard

ISBN: 1537742477
ISBN-13: 978-1537742472

Table of Contents

Introduction

I want to thank you and congratulate you for downloading the book *Hillary Clinton: Truth and Lies.*

This book contains proven steps and strategies on how to become a truly knowledgeable voter with regard to the Democratic nominee Hillary Clinton. Clinton has been under fire from the beginning of her political career to the present for lying and breaking the rules. Making a decision about whom to vote for in this year's election is a personal thing, yet it can impact us all for at least the next four years.

Here's an inescapable fact: Hillary Clinton has already made history as the first female presidential nominee of any party. Clinton has also earned a negative reputation resulting from scandals and cover-ups in her own personal pursuit of power and money. You need to gain valuable and critical insight into the mindset of this candidate before you decide to vote for her.

If you do not develop your ability to gain critical insight into how Hillary Clinton makes judgments in her thought process and recognize the patterns of her deceit before the fall elections, you may find you voted for the wrong candidate after it's too late. It is your duty as an American citizen to be well-informed.

It's time for you to become an amazing expert in assessing the mental consistencies demonstrated by this fascinating candidate who has over twenty years' experience in key areas of the political framework of this country. History has documented the role of Hillary Clinton in a number of scandals that have cost this country the lives of its citizens, compromised national security, and spent many millions of taxpayer dollars for investigations. Your vote has value; don't give it away without knowing the facts!

Chapter 1: Truth, Lies, and Politics

The main questions that must be asked are simple. What is the truth? What is a lie? Any child can tell you the difference. Somehow, as we age, we come to believe that when educated, wealthy individuals or people shown in the media tell us something we should automatically believe it as truth. We all know the difference between right and wrong. Once a person lies to you, do you ever trust them again?

For years, people have been saying they don't believe half of what they see or hear and for good reason. Everyone has an agenda that they are trying to push. Politicians try and push their policies. Advertisements try and push their products.

Politicians make empty promises all the time; it's the status quo of the business. Are empty promises lies? Most people agree that they are.

Is being in denial the same as lying? This is a different way of looking at the concept, but the answer again is yes. Proving it in an investigation is something different.

When we are talking about running the country, is telling a "white lie" bad? Remember, we're not talking about if you liked grandma's soup or not. Dishonest behavior exhibited by anyone is a red flag and warrants close attention.

Psychology

Facts help your intuition. We've often heard that "if something sounds too good to be true, then it usually is" works well in these cases. Sometimes you just have a feeling but no proof, until one day you notice a fact that substantiates your feeling.

A proven strategy is to approach issues from the common sense side of our brains. By not thinking clearly and making sound decisions it is no wonder we are labeled by foreign countries as being led along unassumingly like sheep.

Salespeople and politicians both use the psychology of the mind to make you buy into what they are selling. They tell you what you want to hear. Political candidates are trying to sell you on electing them, often belittling their opponent in the process.

The Power of the Media

When you turn on the news, you see a person telling you something, and you believe it. How many times have you heard someone say, "I can't believe it's raining? The weatherman said it was supposed to be sunny today." As if it's his fault it rained because he said it would be sunny the day before on television. Watching people in groups lie to each other to get rewarded on reality shows makes the public think this is okay to do in everyday life. This is very powerful stuff.

Lawyers

Being an attorney was considered the most noble profession up until about 75 years ago. Contemporary times say lawyers are liars with a license to steal. Many have a bad reputation and are labeled "ambulance chasers," always looking for other people's money.

People become lawyers to make money. Some practice law while others get into politics. In both cases, you need to have an ego to get to the top. It's a power trip. You need to exaggerate and embellish yourself to stand out and look better than you are, otherwise you become an also-ran.

Why do lawyers get into politics? Many lawyers leave practice to enter politics using the connections they have to form new relationships with businesses and high-ranking individuals, all in the name of money and power.

As a lawyer, Hillary knows the rules and, more importantly, how to break them.

Politicians

Once upon a time, in the early years of the government of this country, politicians had other vocations and being involved in government positions was a side job with no benefits. The corruption began when they became full-time positions with all the "perks."

Politicians usually have a legal background they use as a stepping stone to catapult them into the political arena. Their knowledge of the law makes them ripe for this profession in view of those who elected them. Their familiarity with the law allows them an advantage when discussing bills to be passed.

It's amazing how the current crop of politicians have previous involvement in dirty deeds of the past. It seems to suggest some sort of nepotism/incestuous clan where politicos get recycled. This has been going on for years.

The popular consensus is that they don't serve the people that elected them, they serve themselves.

Elections

The goal in politics is for a candidate to win the election. The powerful money backing the candidates with donations, also known as "big business" of some kind (like big pharma) and special interest groups, put pressure on their candidate to win at all costs and by any means necessary. So what are we as citizens supposed to do? All the static around us in the form of distractions are taking our thinking away from the matters that really count. Are we told the truth from the media, or is it slanted?

Politicians in general have been labeled as liars since pretty much the dawn of government. Not one politician in contemporary times who told the truth and followed through one hundred percent of the time comes to mind. Honor and respect don't exist. It's business as usual. That is how everyone perceives the system.

Dodging questions with a lot of words that say nothing is common—just like any speech from a veteran political figure who is trying to force a cover-up of something they did wrong.

You can't make an omelet without breaking some eggs. Doing damage to your opponent to get what you want is considered appropriate in politics.

Government

Supposedly, we voluntarily elect our government officials in this country. Historically, it is based on choosing a candidate for the government of the people, by the people, and for the people.

It is a fact; history is written by the victors. Before democracy, those with the most power ruled. It was called "might makes right" when bullies ruled. Then we became civilized and decided to vote for folks to represent us. People who supposedly were very knowledgeable and had the best interests in mind of the people they represented in a party.

Ethics is a big issue; not surprisingly, there is a committee on this. It's to protect the people from the officials they elected and to maintain order where finances are exchanged. This can be seen mostly in banking and insurance.

Mudslinging - Dirty Politics

Even the accusations about Hillary's opponents are lies. Conjuring up stories about your opponents is all part of the game, but Hillary is taking this to a new level in her campaign. At this time, she doesn't have as much mud to sling since she is in a compromised position from the resulting email debacle and her acceptance of Bill's womanizing behavior.

Chapter 2: Hillary History

Early Years

Born Hillary Rodham, she grew up in Park Ridge, Illinois, in a conservative republican household. A demonstrated achievement-oriented student, she graduated high school in the top five percent of her class. In 1969, she graduated from Wellesley College with a BA in political science along with departmental honors. From there she went on to Yale Law School where she met Bill Clinton. After earning her JD in 1973, she began postgraduate work and, in 1974, served as a member of the impeachment inquiry staff during Watergate.

Political Party

With her father Hugh Rodham being a staunch republican and supporter of Barry Goldwater, Hillary began as a supporter of that party. This would continue until, while in college, she came to dislike how the Nixon campaign portrayed Rockefeller at the Republican National Convention in 1968. She has been a democrat ever since.

Mindset Formatives

We all admire and are influenced by people, mostly as we are growing up but even in adulthood. They help form who we become. It was natural for her to start out as a republican since that was her initial exposure growing up. She shows her independence and ability to form her own opinion in time. It is interesting to note two people who Hillary Clinton says she admired, Margaret Sanger and Saul Alinsky, and to see now how they influenced her mindset today. Both were outspoken public figures who were involved in thrusting change upon the world, albeit for very different reasons. The basis of the power to move people in certain directions is what Hillary is all about.

Margaret Sanger

Sanger was an early eugenics advocate, feminist, racist, and founder of Planned Parenthood. Her writings reveal the lifelong passion of her beliefs. Hillary has, on more than one occasion, stated she admired Sanger's life and leadership and viewed it as a time that was the most transformational in human history. It is apparent that through the power of political leadership, Hillary wants to make history. She wants to transform society through her political power. An example is her attempt at Healthcare Reform in 1993. Along with that power comes big money, which we have seen is a motivator as well.

Saul Alinsky

Another individual who served to influence Hillary's mindset during her formative years was Saul Alinsky. One must remember the youth of the 1960s and their radical nature.

Alinsky was an author, radical activist, and community organizer. He moved people and genuinely tried to help the poor and minorities organize to be heard, not ignored. His method was one of pushing to new ground gradually in order to make changes.

Hillary wrote a 92-page senior thesis titled "There Is Only the Fight..." on what she learned from him as she admired the veracity of his beliefs which affected her philosophically. She spoke to him, and they corresponded at length where he even offered her a job (that she declined). It was from him that she became excited about fighting for the causes she believed in, but using her own methodology. The thesis was suppressed by the White House when Hillary became First Lady as it did not want to reveal her extremist and radical views to the world—views that she apparently still has today. Also, it is only available on microfilm that needs to be signed out and not on the internet.

It is apparent in the tone of Hillary's public commentary that she has become her own version of the modern-day crusader, saying she wants what's best for the people, but in the background is brandishing her own agenda. She is intelligent and shrewd but has flaws like everyone else. We find her ambition to transform the public in these contemporary times. She wants to change the system from the inside. That has always been her goal as will be seen in later chapters.

Career Path

After Watergate, she married Bill and soon after co-founded Arkansas Advocates for Children and Families. She was appointed the first female chair of the Legal Services Corporation before becoming a partner at the Rose Law Firm, and ultimately, First Lady of Arkansas.

First Lady and Beyond

While Bill Clinton was running for president back in 1992, he made the comment that if he were to become president, the country would be getting "two for one." At the time, it was taken to mean she would be an involved First Lady and that there would be two knowledgeable, politically savvy, and capable individuals who would share in running the country. Today, looking back, we wonder if he meant that voting him into the presidency back then would be a vote for her in the future.

People often used the term "Billary" from 1993 to 2000, referring to Hillary making decisions for Bill and that she was calling the shots from the background to a degree. The reason they have stayed together is that they complement each other so well. It is clear from the first days of Bill's first term that the presidency was a joint venture between them. She was put in charge of projects, but they were not without issue.

The dossier on Hillary's whole life has been about ambition and getting to the top. She only cares about what she wants, not how she gets it or who falls by the wayside. A number of people who were at odds with Hillary Clinton have died under mysterious circumstances. Thank goodness for the internet saving these bits of history that many forgot or did not know happened during the past 38 years while Hillary was involved in politics.

It's scary the way she lies to the public with such apparent ease, but those lies are starting to catch up with her as evidenced by her low ratings as the 2016 election approaches.

Personality

Much of what you will see in this book has to do with Hillary Clinton's aggressive goals to succeed. Her drive shows through on all counts throughout her career. The deaths, although not directly committed by her, resulted from scandals she was part of and possibly masterminded. There are many of them that occurred over time and have seemed to come about at just the right time as to stifle a testimony or cause a distraction from another scandal.

Her scandals are like drunk driving; it's been done 100 times, but you only need to get caught once to be labeled. Those who get caught have usually done it many times. Even those that get caught often become repeat offenders. They can't stop, and she won't stop. Whether she becomes president or not, there will be other fiascos down the road; it's a part of her, it's who and what she is.

Her reactions to being told she lied or broke the rules are childish. She never apologizes, but instead, says she made a mistake. No one should think they are above the law. When reprimanded for wrongdoings she either says she made a mistake or maintains silence in the hope it will go away and just blow over so that she can move on. Others around her get fired for making smaller mistakes.

As any Sherlock Holmes fan knows, the criminal mind has been said to be a very intelligent, devious, cunning, cold-hearted, and calculating one. Criminals always continue until they are apprehended by the authorities, they just don't stop on their own. Their greed keeps them going like an addiction to a drug, and the crimes become more intense to keep getting that high level of satisfaction.

In the end, Hillary will reach a breaking point, and her undoing will be the enormity of all the scandals put together, the weight of which is undeniable.

Chapter 3: Watergate

The Democratic National Committee (DNC) headquarters was located at the Watergate office complex in Washington, D.C.

In 1972, there was a break-in at the DNC and five men were arrested. The investigation revealed evidence that the Nixon administration was involved and that President Nixon himself had recorded conversations in his offices and had attempted a cover-up which was leading to his impeachment, but he resigned in disgrace before impeachment proceedings could be finalized.

A short time after Hillary graduated from Yale Law School she was hired as a staff attorney for the House Judiciary Committee investigating the Watergate scandal.

Jerome Zeifman was assigned as Chief Counsel by his boss at the time, Judiciary Committee Chairman Peter Rodino. It was Rodino who was also the boss of Impeachment Inquiry Special Counsel John Doar. It was Doar who directly supervised Hillary's work.

Zeifman claims he kept a diary of events from Watergate. In it, he maintains he would not give Hillary a recommendation claiming she "[lied, was dishonest, and was unethical.]" This stems from Hillary, having followed orders from Rodino through her supervisor Doar, who took files without questioning an assignment to create a brief that addressed whether Nixon had the right to representation by counsel at evidentiary hearings. Obviously, having honor and showing respect for the process to be done correctly were not issues for her.

Hillary was not fired as was frequently mentioned by famous radio talk show host Rush Limbaugh. Zeifman has been interviewed about his recollections working with Hillary and throughout he has critiqued her in a negative manner. In his book *Without Honor: The Impeachment of President Nixon and the Crimes of Camelot* released in 1998, Zeifman basically states Hillary did not know what she was doing.

After the impeachment inquiry had disbanded, Hillary failed the District of Columbia Bar, but had passed the Arkansas Bar and went to Arkansas to be with her future husband, Bill Clinton.

Subsequent chapters will discuss her involvement in many other investigations, both while in the White House and after.

What can be seen from Hillary's work at Watergate is that it illustrates her cool disregard for the rules early on in her fledgling career just out of law school. There does not seem to be any moral question as to whether she was involved in doing something wrong.

Chapter 4: Whitewater

The Whitewater case began in 1994. In actuality, Whitewater came about from another investigation that was being done regarding the collapse of a financial institution by the name of Madison Guaranty Savings and Loan run by James McDougal. In looking for witnesses to the bank's failure, the names of Bill and Hillary Clinton stood out when David Hale testified.

Hale contended Bill pressured him for a $300,000 loan for the Whitewater investment, but did not want to be named in the transaction. It was Hale's second round of testimony that uncovered the Clintons.

From there it just opened up and proceeded to quickly uncover a series of scandals involving the Clintons. Whitewater was Hillary's first noted involvement in a criminal investigation, but it would not be her last.

In short, Whitewater was an Ozark Mountain property investment failure originated in 1978 by the Clintons and their partners in the deal, the McDougals.

The allegation was regarding a fraudulent loan made to Susan McDougal's marketing company to pay off the debts owed by the two couples.

Independent Counsel Kenneth Starr led the investigation. With new twists and turns it took all of eight years and millions in taxpayer money to sort out the Whitewater probe.

In the end, the Clintons were never prosecuted, but their knowledge and involvement in Whitewater did open the door to other investigations of both Bill and Hillary. The most notable of these will be explored with relevant detail in the subsequent chapters of this book.

The significance of Whitewater is twofold. First, it served to be like a big ball of connected strings, and when unraveled by the investigation showed a slew of other controversies with the Clintons attached to each one in some way. It was like every mistake they made professionally had been connected like a chain.

Second, it documents Hillary Clinton's personal agenda of doing and saying whatever it takes to prosper.

Apparently, copies of 115 pages of "missing" Rose Law Firm billing records were found in the White House in 1996, but the originals are still missing. They reveal how she had repeatedly met with key figures involved in the Whitewater fiasco. It is interesting to see a common theme of documents gone missing that could be used as evidence to bring charges against her. This is the sign of a true lawyer.

Chapter 5: Pardongate

Before President Bill Clinton's second term was to officially expire in 2001, he granted 176 presidential pardons, many of which were signed on his last day in office. These pardons drew a firestorm of controversy because of some of the large financial contributions that were made prior to the pardons. Accusations of using his position for personal gain have been nothing new to Bill, but this put a whole new label on the term "corruption."

Hillary Senate Contributions - Cash for Pardons

One such example is Marc Rich, who was convicted of tax evasion. Rich was indicted on 50 counts of fraud, trading with Iran during the U.S. Embassy hostage crisis, racketeering, and evading more than $48 million in income taxes. All combined, these crimes totaled 300 years in prison.

After indicted, Rich fled the country to Switzerland. His actions put him on the FBI's Most Wanted list. His wife's contributions to the Clinton Presidential library and Hillary's 2000 Senate campaign were significant. He remained in Switzerland until President Clinton pardoned him. Apparently, everyone has a price.

There was an alleged scheme made by Hillary's brothers, Hugh and Tony Rodham, who were purportedly taking money in return for promising presidential pardons.

Carlos Vignali was a convicted drug kingpin serving the sixth of his 15-year term when he was pardoned. Reportedly, Hillary's brother Hugh received large sums for being pardoned which was said to be "very important" to Hillary. It is interesting to note the Vignali family is involved in major real estate transaction business in the Los Angeles, California, area.

Almost ironically, Susan McDougal from the Whitewater scandal was pardoned as was Bill's half-brother Robert for drug charges.

The case involving swindler Glenn Braswell, who was sentenced to three years in prison, was another pardon granted by Bill Clinton. Hugh Rodham was paid hundreds of thousands for a pardon granted by Bill on his last day in office.

Chapter 6: Cattle Futures Trading

One of the items uncovered during Whitewater was a controversial futures trading set of transactions made by Hillary. Futures trading is very risky and speculative; you need to know what you are doing. It also has to be clear that you can lose more money than you invest. Hillary's stated objective was to build financial security and a nest egg.

In 1978, around the same time the Whitewater investment took place, Hillary decided to invest $1,000 in cattle futures trading. Even though the minimum investment required was higher, she still managed to open an account. Her friends who knew her at the brokerage made an exception, and she bought on margin. Just ten months later she cashed out, having amassed about $100,000 by mid-1979.

She claims to have schooled herself by studying the market, reading everything she could, and talking to people. Although a very intelligent person, futures investing is complex and, like poker, you can learn the rudiments in about an hour, but it takes years to become proficient. She does admit to both making and losing money during this time, but coming out ahead in the end.

The interesting, and suspicious, piece is that she was steered into this by a friend and fellow lawyer, James Blair, who just happened to be employed as outside counsel to Tyson Foods, which was Arkansas's largest employer at that time. Blair had done very well for himself as a futures trader since 1977 and was forever telling friends about his success in that market.

Also of interest is that the broker to Blair and Hillary Clinton was Robert L. "Red" Bone, manager at Refco, who was under investigation at the time for records violations. A recurring theme is how almost all the people Hillary does business with get investigated. Bone was Blair's legal client and had also been a former executive at Tyson Foods.

The main issue is whether her trading success was skill, luck, inside information, or a scandal of leveraging trades by the key players involved. Skilled investors know it is difficult for a novice to make such a rate of return in such a short period of time. Veteran investor analysts agree that her timing was perfect to catch the biggest cattle boom in history. Oddly enough, she never invested in futures again, saying it was nerve-racking and that she no longer had the stomach for it.

The truth is she made a lot of money in a short period of time, even though there are records showing she did lose in some trades. Whether she did so legally and played by the rules could not be proven one way or the other, but it's a very hard sell for most people to believe.

If she lied about her trading success and profited, this was indeed unethical. Nothing could be proven about the mechanics of what transpired, only her involvement.

Since all of this was discovered in 1994, some 15 years had elapsed, which was well past the statute of limitations. Another case of how convenient it was for her.

As a result, officially, there was never any investigation or charges made against Hillary Clinton. It was her money that was at risk and, during the 10-month period in question, she came out ahead.

Chapter 7: Vincent W. Foster Jr.

The Whitewater investigation led to many different scandals. As evidence was being uncovered, pressure was growing within the White House to deliver any information it had. Deputy White House Counsel Vince Foster, a close friend and business partner to Hillary, was in charge of finding and providing that information. As he was in the process of doing his duty, something happened that would forever leave a blemish on the Clinton Administration—Vince Foster allegedly committed suicide.

Background

Vince Foster was an early childhood friend of Bill Clinton. They lived across the street from each other, and later Foster was the Deputy White House Counsel at Bill's request during his initial term as president. Before this, Foster was a partner at the Rose Law Firm and was both a colleague and good friend of Hillary and the family.

All those who knew him say he was a good, honest person who enjoyed his successful career practicing law. He was a former military man, an excellent student and athlete, and president of his graduating class—an outstanding human being on all counts, a perfect front man. Then something went wrong.

Suicide

The suicide in 1993 was from an alleged self-inflicted gunshot wound to the mouth. A torn-up resignation note was found in his briefcase that was missing the piece where his signature should have gone. It is not really clear that it was a suicide note. He was said to have allegedly been suffering from clinical depression for which he was taking medication. It was said he was unhappy with his work in politics and Washington in general.

It should also be noted that just before his death Foster was to be called to testify by Kenneth Starr regarding Whitewater.

Even though no fewer than five investigations were done to confirm suicide from a self-inflicted gunshot wound to the mouth as the manner of death, theories of a cover-up persisted through three years of investigation by Kenneth Starr as part of Whitewater. The conspiracy idea was alleged to damage Bill Clinton. The theory is that Foster knew too much about the Clintons, so he had to pay the ultimate price.

Aftermath

It is alleged, on the night of Foster's death, Hillary had sent Maggie Williams (the First Lady's Chief of Staff), Patsy Thomasson (White House Administration), and Craig Livingston (Director of White House Security) to illegally enter into Foster's office to steal documents even though White House Counsel Bernard Nussbaum barred anyone from going into the office for any reason. The specific documents targeted were any and all those pertaining to Whitewater and Travelgate showing suspicious Clinton involvement, even going so far as to erase memos with Hillary's initials on them.

After Foster's death, $2.73 million was found in a Swiss bank account, with the account number found in his wallet. It is contended he took money on the side for a cover-up. This is hardly likely since Foster was making $300,000 at his Arkansas law firm as a partner. This was a job he actually liked and planned to go back to after his time in the White House. It is believed this was planted as a way to discredit this very credible man. The paper with the account number could have easily been put in his wallet after his death.

Enter Miguel Rodriguez

Miguel Rodriguez was brought in as the lead investigator for the Office of the Independent Counsel investigating the death of Vince Foster.

From the very beginning, the evidence he found in the investigation did not add up. Rodriguez did not believe Foster's death to be a suicide. Allegedly, Foster was killed, and his murder was made to look like a suicide.

A bullet hole was also found in his neck, but not reported originally. Even after it was found, the evidence went missing and even today only the single shot to the mouth is blamed for his death. Crime scene photos were doctored to look like a suicide. Falsification of records surfaced, and witness intimidation, tampering, and destruction of evidence were all found by Rodriguez. His best attempts to expose the cover-up fell on deaf ears as no one, especially the Clintons, wanted to believe it was anything more than a suicide.

Ultimately, in disgust, he resigned.

The Motive

The motive for him being killed was that he was an honest person who knew too much about the Clintons. Theorists feel that his testimony would be damaging to his friends and the Clintons. The bottom line from what can be deciphered is that they knew each other and they asked him to take the job. Foster had a good work ethic and he was a trusted friend of the Clintons. But Foster hated the job and working for Hillary, who was now saturated with power, bossy, and mean. The ripped-up pieces of the note found in his briefcase show his dismay if it is real. No signature for the note was ever found. There was a missing piece where his signature should have been. That leads us back to whether the note was real.

This shameful and illegal cover-up most assuredly underscores Hillary Clinton's "win at any cost" attitude and does not put her outside the premise of murdering Vince Foster. It would seem that it was coming down to him or them, and he was out.

Vince and Hillary

Questions about a romantic relationship between Hillary and Vince have come up, but most dismiss it only remarking that Vince seemed to fill the role of the "emotional husband" in Hillary's life. From all accounts, they were close friends and business partners.

Hillary's relationships should only be viewed from the establishment of her mental arrangement to get ahead at all costs and feed her desire for power—that is, if she were to be unfaithful in a relationship with a man it wouldn't matter as long as it served her purpose.

It is evident from her beginning with Watergate that she will do whatever she needs to prop herself up and succeed, even if it means sabotaging others.

Her goal is to become president where she thinks she will be able to absolve herself from all her wrongdoings with the attitude of "If I'm president, I can't be all that bad." Just like as the presidential candidate she thinks that by getting this far she is in the clear. Be sure and watch those around her to see who will take the fall next as the scapegoat. Democratic National Convention Chair Wasserman Shultz lost her job in the summer of 2016 after it was revealed that the Democratic Party headquarters was hacked and thousands of documents were leaked out including several damaging emails about Hillary.

Chapter 8: Bill's Indiscretions

When Hillary was the Senator of New York, she released an autobiography titled *Living History*, released in 2003. She chose to be interviewed by Barbara Walters in a one-hour televised special program. The big question was regarding her relationship with her husband who had an affair with Monica Lewinsky. Hillary stated that even though she was furious that Bill did this to her and disrespected their family in front of the country, she still thought of him highly and added that after deep thought and counseling, she decided to forgive him and hoped they could grow old together.

The television special served three things: the first was to promote the book, the second showed her forgiving nature, and the third was to open the door and let people know she would consider running for president in 2008.

Hillary spoke to the BBC about how forgiving Bill was the right choice for her and added that when making a decision such as this, one must consider the personal and professional aspects of life. The takeaway message was, in essence, saying that the image of keeping the family unit together was more appealing to voters. The psychology of stressing forgiveness with family worked because her popularity ratings started to increase. This helped her become the U.S. Senator of New York, but more importantly, she became the star of the Clinton power couple.

In fact, she goes on to explain how historical writing, cultures, and religion convey how liberating it feels to forgive someone, possibly more than for the one being forgiven.

Hillary and Bill met in law school when they were at Yale. She quickly recognized the Rhodes Scholar's womanizing ways. Hillary also noted they formed a very compatible couple. She was serious and focused on the tasks at hand teaching him discipline, while he was more eager to socialize and develop relationships. Bill proposed to Hillary following their graduation. Hillary declined.

She loved him, saw his future potential, and decided to disregard his indiscretions that she knew would continue. She realized her long-term future success was linked to his, and that they complemented each other—that together she could achieve the place in life where she wanted to be in this world. Accepting another proposal, they married in 1975.

When the public found out about all the affairs, she forgave him every time despite the embarrassment and it kept his public approval afloat—simply by virtue of her forgiveness of him.

When the Clintons left the White House at the end of Bill's second term, Hillary's approval rating was at an all-time high. After the 2008 election, she took the post as Secretary of State at the request of President Barack Obama.

Hillary's personal life is a key part of her political life. Should Hillary become president, Bill would become the first First Husband in the history of the White House.

Bill Clinton

Although this book is about Hillary Clinton and the lies she perpetrates in cover-ups to advance her political career, it must be noted her husband was the center of many damaging allegations which will briefly be discussed here. In return, Hillary has since used Bill's influence to offset and minimize charges against her.

The former 42nd President of the United States has the distinction of having been accused by several women of sexual assault. It is interesting to note that almost all of these allegations surfaced only after he attained the position of president and that the alleged victims have been harassed as a result of coming forth.

By no means is this a complete list. Here are a number of historical allegations of indecent incidents:

In 1969, Eileen Wellstone was 19 when she met Bill at a pub near Oxford while he was a student there. She claims sexual assault. A retired State Department employee confirmed that he spoke with the girl's family and filed a report. Bill Clinton admitted to having sex with her claiming it was consensual. Amazingly, the girl's family declined to press charges.

In 1972, a 22-year-old woman, who requested to remain anonymous, told campus police at Yale University that she was sexually assaulted by Bill Clinton at the college, but no charges were ever filed.

In 1974, a female student, who has declined to go on record, at the University of Arkansas alleged that her law school instructor Bill Clinton tried to prevent her from leaving his office. She stated he groped her and forced his hand inside her blouse. She complained to her advisor who confronted Bill Clinton, who asserted the student initiated acts with him. Shortly after the incident, the student left the school. There have also been several other former students that have confirmed the incident in confidential interviews and stated there were other reports of Bill Clinton attempting to force himself on female students.

In 1978, Juanita Broaddrick, a volunteer in Bill Clinton's campaign for governor, said he brutally raped her. White House attorneys report this was consensual.

From 1978-1980, state troopers who were assigned to protect Governor Clinton were aware of at least seven complaints from women on whom Bill Clinton forced himself or attempted to use force sexually. One former trooper told how they would escort women to Bill Clinton's hotel room after political events, frequently more than one in an evening.

In 1979, Carolyn Moffet met Bill Clinton at a political fundraiser and then got invited to meet the Governor at his hotel room. She was escorted to his hotel room by a state trooper and, when in the room, saw him sitting on a couch wearing only an undershirt. He allegedly pointed to his genitalia and ordered her to engage in oral sex. She refused, and he became angry grabbing her head and forcing it into his lap. She pulled away and ran from the room. A former neighbor of hers said afterward she would receive harassing phone calls.

Elizabeth Ward was a Miss Arkansas who won Miss America in 1982. She told her friends she was forced to have sex with Bill Clinton. Ward, now married, told an interviewer she did have consensual sex with Bill Clinton, but close friends of Ward maintain she privately feels he forced himself on her.

Paula Jones worked as an Arkansas state worker. She filed a sexual harassment case against Bill Clinton after the then-Governor made a demand for oral sex in a Little Rock hotel room. Bill Clinton settled the case with Jones in 1998 for an $850,000 cash payment, which just goes to prove it really happened and he wanted it to go away.

Sandra Allen James claims she was invited to Bill Clinton's hotel room (is there a trend here?) where he pinned her to the wall while he stuck his hand up her dress. At this point, she screamed so loud the state trooper stationed outside the door banged on it asking if everything was all okay. Bill Clinton then released her, and she ran out of the room. She reported the incident to her boss who advised her to keep quiet if she wanted to keep her job. She says she later learned other women suffered the same fate. She allegedly would not go forward claiming the Clinton White House destroys people who get in their way.

In 1992, Christy Zercher was a flight attendant on a leased campaign plane. She says Bill exposed himself to her and grabbed her breasts while making explicit remarks about oral sex. An ABC News video on the plane shows an inebriated Bill Clinton with his hand between another flight attendant's legs. Zercher said White House attorney Bruce Lindsey pressured her not to go public about the assault.

In 1993, Kathleen Willey was a White House volunteer who reported that Bill Clinton grabbed her, fondled her breast, and pressed her hand against his genitals. She told her story in a *60 Minutes* interview and alleged she became a target of a White House-directed smear campaign after going public.

Over 30 interviews were made with former state troopers, retired Arkansas state employees, and former University of Arkansas and Yale students who refuse to go public out of fear.

The resounding tone is that Bill has a problem treating women as sex toys for his pleasure. He does whatever he wants, and Hillary does her best to help cover up for the sake of power and greed. This truly is a marriage of convenience.

Retaliation Detailed

In retaliation for making accusations about the indecent assault, the Clintons have been said to have hired private investigators to try and expose their adversaries. Threats, scare tactics, and stalking have been confirmed by a number of the former accusers who have been willing to come forth and speak out about the unfairness.

It is asserted that Hillary orchestrated a campaign of harassment and intimidation that fits a pattern described by other women.

The only allegations Bill admits to are the affairs with Gennifer Flowers and Monica Lewinsky.

Mistakes were made by the accuser Broaddrick, who continued to support Bill Clinton at public events after being raped. Broaddrick also had signed a statement saying she did not have sex with Bill Clinton. Afterward, she said she did not want to testify publicly about the details of such a horrific event.

Broaddrick resurfaced with Hillary's 2016 presidential campaign stating Hillary knew what happened and how she threatened Broaddrick to keep silent. Broaddrick gave interviews in 2015 because she was angered by Hillary's statements that victims of sexual crimes should be believed. To Broaddrick, there was the public side of Hillary and the dark side that she faced when she went public.

Dolly Kyle Browning, a lawyer in Texas, made a deposition as part of the Paula Jones case. She was a childhood classmate of Bill and knew him since age 11. She also had an affair with him for approximately 18 years. When she began writing a novel that outlined the affair, she alleged Bill tried to halt its publication.

The Paula Jones case against Bill alleging sexual harassment is what put him under oath to testify about his sexual history. It was here he denied having had an affair with Monica Lewinsky. This denial is what led to his impeachment for perjury and obstruction of justice.

In 1998, Kathleen Willey came forth in the Paula Jones case and alleged Bill Clinton assaulted her in the White House in 1993. Kenneth Starr granted her immunity for her testimony in his separate inquiry.

Linda Tripp, a White House staffer, testified that Willey's sexual contact with Bill Clinton was consensual. Almost ironically, Willey's second husband, Edward E. Willey Jr., was found dead from a gunshot wound on the exact same day she claimed Bill Clinton's sexual misconduct took place. His death was determined to be a suicide by investigators. She has written a book and been interviewed on *60 Minutes* talking about her suspicions that the Clintons were somehow involved in the death of her former husband, and she details the similarities to the alleged suicide of Vince Foster, including how both deaths occurred in close proximity to each other in the state of Virginia. Kenneth Starr dismissed the Willey case due to insufficient evidence.

During the Paula Jones trial, Gennifer Flowers revealed her 12-year affair with Bill, who testified under oath that he had sexual relations with her. For once he came clean.

Other allegations have come out with all of them saying the same thing over and over which is that Bill had relationships with them or had propositioned them. He is often labeled as a predator, but perhaps a better label for him would be a sex addict who needs professional help.

Hillary has been shown as an accessory in that she knew about the misconduct but did nothing, thus serving as an enabler. He knew he could do it and that she would help cover for him without question. Given this fact, and that everyone in the country has seen the stories of Bill's "exploits" on television, it's a wonder people believe her rantings about fairness for women involved in sexual assault allegations.

In his defense, Hillary also uses religion to compare Bill to the Prodigal Son—that he may be taken back despite his indiscretions. Even though the public has passed their judgment on Bill over the decades, she still stands behind him, at least when in public view.

How a woman can remain with and be supportive of a man who has done what he has, repeatedly, raises questions of motive. There are more reports than the ones listed here showing dozens upon dozens of women, most of whom want to remain nameless, who have suffered by his aggressions. It is likely that Hillary may need Bill more than Bill needs Hillary. Bill has always been a better campaigner than Hillary. But this time, it is Hillary that wants to get elected. That may be one of the driving forces that keeps them together. It seems less likely that she would be able to run for president as a divorced woman. There is also, of course, the power and money that they share through the Clinton Foundation. That may be another factor that keeps them together.

Chapter 9: Using the IRS

The Internal Revenue Service may have been used, or abused, for corrupt means and to harass political enemies. Back in the day, tax evasion was what they used to convict Al Capone.

Audit Your Enemies

During Bill Clinton's terms in office, the IRS conducted audits against individuals and groups who had brought either legal scandals to light for the Administration or had criticized the President or his policies.

Among the groups audited were the National Rifle Association, the Heritage Foundation, the Concerned Women of America, National Review, Citizens Against Government Waste, the National Center for Public Policy Research, American Spectator (which was burglarized three times), the American Policy Center, Citizens for Honest Government, the American Cause, David Horowitz's Center for the Study of Popular Culture, the Progress & Freedom Foundation, and the Western Journalism Center.

Individuals who were audited after they went public against Clinton include ex-lovers Liz Ward Gracen and Gennifer Flowers, sexual assault accusers Juanita Broaddrick and Paula Jones, Bill Dale, a fired White House Travel Office Director; and attorney Kent Masterson Brown. Bill O'Reilly of FOX News and critic of the Clintons said he was audited three times.

IRS Under Obama

When Hillary served under Obama as Secretary of State, Obama may have learned from Hillary how to use the IRS. The Obama Administration seems to have done a much better job of utilizing the IRS for attacking the Tea Party Republicans than the Clintons ever did. The Obama Administration used the power of the IRS to prevent the formation of Tea Party organizations for years. If a group cannot operate, it simply cannot be effective.

Chapter 10: Healthcare Reform 1993

In his quest for the presidency during his 1992 campaign, Bill Clinton focused on a healthcare reform package that would provide healthcare to all Americans.

Immediately after being sworn into office in 1993, the first steps were put into motion for The Clinton Health Care Plan. Bill set up the Task Force on National Health Care Reform and appointed Hillary as the Chair to devise and implement the plan.

The idea was to mandate employers to provide coverage to all their employees through closely regulated health maintenance organizations (HMOs). Controversial processes surfaced and resulted in litigation primarily from the Association of American Physicians and Surgeons.

In short, the bill was over 1,000 pages long and required each U.S. citizen and permanent resident alien to be enrolled in one of the qualified health plans. Dis-enrollment was forbidden until coverage was in place by another plan to ensure there was continuous coverage. It also listed the coverage and annual out-of-pocket expenses for each plan with the provision there would be no cost for people below a certain set income level. The act listed funding to be allocated to the states for the administration of this plan, beginning at 38.3 billion in 2003.

Secrets Behind Closed Doors

In 1993, Hillary was involved in litigation over secret proceedings. The exact details of these closed-door meetings of the Health Care Task Force have never been revealed. The U.S. Court of Appeals for the D.C. Circuit reviewed the issue of whether Hillary was in violation of the Federal Advisory Committee Act (FACA) which requires openness in affairs where the government is involved. The White House argued that Article II of the U.S. Constitution made it unconstitutional to apply FACA to her involvement with the Task Force. Ultimately, she was absolved, in that, as First Lady, she was no longer a private citizen, but a government official.

In February 1993, a lawsuit was filed against Hillary by the Association of American Physicians and Surgeons (AAPS) and several other groups with a vested interest in gaining access to the list of task force members. This information was released when the AAPS won and in addition, they were awarded a sum to cover their legal costs in the suit.

The End Result

Opponents criticized the bill as restrictive of patient choice and overly bureaucratic, unofficially calling it "Hillarycare" due to her involvement as Task Force Chair.

Failure

By September 1994, Senate Majority Leader George J. Mitchell tried a final compromise to save the bill. The plan had failed. With the plan scrapped, Bill Clinton's political position was weakened. This was a major blow for both Bill and Hillary.

Chapter 11: Chinagate

Chinagate, which is part of Commercegate, was a campaign fundraising scandal in which Hillary was very involved.

Re-election Funding

When Bill was running for re-election in 1996, he was the recipient of large sums of donations by high-tech companies eager to do business with China. The premise is that they also took bribes from the Chinese who were interested in opening the door to high-tech information as well.

A scheme allegedly cooked up by Hillary was for then-Secretary of Commerce Ron Brown to sell seats, under the guise of campaign contributions, on taxpayer-funded trade missions. Judicial Watch, a conservative organization, brought a legal case seeking to find out the truth about Chinagate. The Clinton Administration sought to destroy documents related to Chinagate so that Judicial Watch would not find any smoking gun.

Confidante and business partner to Ron Brown, Nolanda Hill, testified in court that Hillary Clinton was the mastermind behind a scheme to sell seats for campaign contributions on China trade missions that Secretary Ron Brown was to organize through the commerce department. Further, Nolanda Hill said that the Clinton Administration told Brown to delay the case by withholding sensitive documents before the 1996 elections and to find a way not to comply with the court's orders.

There were numerous investigations into Chinagate: congressional, Justice Department, Federal Election Commission, and FBI cases. Ron Brown's Commerce Department and Ron himself were the targets of a number of these investigations. Ron Brown subsequently died on an unrelated commerce trip to Bosnia that Hillary Clinton sent him on. There will be a whole chapter on Ron Brown later in this book.

A larger and more sinister plan was hatched by the Clinton Administration and CEO Bernard Schwartz of Loral Space & Communications Ltd. The plan was to transfer U.S. missile technology to China to help with Bill Clinton's 1996 presidential campaign. Schwartz donated about $1.5 million to democrats including Bill Clinton. In return, Schwartz got approval from the Clinton Administration State Department to have satellites launched from China. The transfer of technology advanced China's missile program by decades and put money into the Clinton-Gore re-election campaign.

Investigations found that Clinton Administration officials had falsified testimony and deliberately destroyed and concealed records regarding the trade missions.

The Department of Justice investigation found that over 100 people that were somehow connected to the scandal had either fled the country or would plead the Fifth Amendment to avoid testifying.

With no evidence, Federal charges of racketeering were never brought.

As the investigation of this scandal was underway, congressional hearings arose until democrats found evidence of illegal republican fundraising and the "new" Monica Lewinsky case was found to distract the country with another one of Bill's juicy sex scandals.

Much later in 2006, an appellate court upheld an award of $900,000 to Judicial Watch as payment for their legal fees to bring this case to court on behalf of Loral shareholders.

Chapter 12: Ronald H. Brown

It was on April 3, 1996, that Commerce Secretary Ron Brown died along with 34 others when their Air Force plane crashed into a mountainside.

Ironically, Hillary had made an unplanned stop in Bosnia a few days before Brown's fatal final flight was to leave that very airport and, there are massive amounts of circumstantial evidence that the Clintons were involved. There is no evidence Islamic or any sort of other terrorists killed Brown, but there is speculation of sabotage from the quick and ineffectual investigation that was done.

The back story is that Brown himself knew too much and was also being investigated for corruption stemming from his involvement in Chinagate. He had damning evidence about all the scandals since Whitewater. He would have been able to provide a direct trail of money which led to Bill and Hillary Clinton. There is even speculation that he confronted the Clintons that he would go public about the Chinagate scandal.

Brown was allegedly Clinton's enforcer with regard to bringing Iranian Muslims and their weapons into the Bosnian war.

The Clintons had ordered Brown to withhold documents requested in the Chinagate investigations. Only weeks before his untimely death, Brown started going to church. When Brown was called to testify in an investigation about himself, he knew he was in serious trouble. He knew the Clintons and what they were capable of. He was scared for his life and the life of Nolanda Hill, his business associate, confidante, and possible lover.

Brown's last days were spent trying to protect his son from going to prison by threatening to expose the White House's unknown Asian (Chinagate) fundraising scheme in which Brown played a major role.

It's clear Brown was pulled into involvement and used like a number of other people as pawns in a scheme put together by Hillary to help Bill. When Bill was out in front as president, she was lurking somewhere in the background making sure any documents or people that could convict them were eliminated to keep control of the power they had and all the money that came with it.

On this trip to Bosnia, Brown was also assigned to broker a deal with the President of Croatia, Franjo Tudjman, and Enron Corporation, as there was big money to be made in getting these two together.

Accident or Assassination?

Here are the facts. Brown's last flight came only six months after the insertion of American troops into Bosnia. The Enron executives had their own plane. The Air Force investigation notes the plane inexplicably deviated almost two miles inland, which is highly unusual. It is the first time the safety portion of the investigation of a downed plane was not allowed to be conducted. Only the accident phase was to be investigated.

There is evidence that the plane lost electrical power when it was seven miles away from where it crashed into the mountains, and the plane was about 2500 feet above the Adriatic Sea. The point at which the electrical power went out was when the plane was flying over water on its approach to Dubrovnik Airport. Why is it believed that there was an electrical power loss in the airplane? There are at least three reasons. First, the tower lost voice contact with the plane. There is a split radar system that watches the approach of the plane. This system uses the transponder of the airplane to track the location of the plane. When the electrical system goes out, the plane transponder also stops. There was a United States AWACS plane in the area that was also tracking Ron Brown's plane by its transponder. The AWACS aircraft stopped tracking Ron Brown's plane at the same time Dubrovnik was not able to track the aircraft. This would seem to rule out a failure of the equipment at Dubrovnik and point to a total electrical failure on the plane. The flight controls and the electrical wires are all run through the same conduit. If the electrical system was disabled for two different systems (voice and transponder), then it is likely that the plane lost flight control as well and just continued on the general course it was on and crashed in the mountains.

The Clinton Administration put out a new story about how the plane crashed in "the worst storm in a decade." This line was picked up by numerous media outlets like *Time* and *Newsweek*. However, the weather was not that bad. There was light rain and visibility of five miles with clouds at 2000 feet.

Three days after the CT-43 crash, the Croatian responsible for the airport's navigation system was found with a bullet to the chest. His death was ruled a suicide. This was only two days before his scheduled interview with the Air Force. There is another theory on how the plane crashed. Sources state the plane was purposely guided into the mountainside. Use of one non-directional beacon to guide the plane from takeoff to a certain area and turn it off when a second beacon would immediately turn on and lead the plane to crash it into the mountainside. The Croatian responsible may have been forced to cooperate at gunpoint and then killed to cover up anything he might say to the U.S. Air Force.

It was reported on Croatian TV and other media that the black boxes from the crashed plane had been recovered and turned over to American authorities. All commercial models of that aircraft come with flight recorders, but the Clinton Administration claimed that this aircraft had no black boxes.

There was a survivor found at the site of the CT-43 (Modified Boeing 737) crash. Shelly Kelly, a stewardess, had survived possibly because she was in the tail of the plane. She was moving and conscious and evacuated by helicopter to a hospital. She was said to have died en route to the hospital, and the cause of death was a broken neck. This was very suspicious, and her death would have been required to cover up what actually happened to the aircraft.

Initial examination of Brown's body by no fewer than three Armed Forces pathologists and a forensic photographer shows a head wound that looks like a bullet hole but with no exit wound. Brown's family was not informed of the matter. Head X-rays were lost. Orders by the Administration were issued such that no autopsy or forensic tests were to be performed. The death certificate notes cause of death as multiple blunt force injuries to the head and Brown was the only one on the flight to have a head wound.

A copy of the head X-rays was discovered by Chris Ruddy when he found Dr. Cogswell was using them as an example in one of the Armed Forces lectures for pathologists. The X-rays clearly showed metal fragments in the brain that were consistent with a gunshot to the top of his head because of the inward beveling hole on the head and the "snowstorm" of metal fragments. When Chris Ruddy started to write articles about the death of Ron Brown, a gag order was placed on Dr. Cogswell and Dr. Hause by the Clinton Administration.

President Clinton ordered the cremation of all victims. This would ensure that any evidence left in the bodies would be destroyed. Bill Clinton also took two days to honor Ron Brown after he died. Nobody would question the possible involvement of one who spends a great deal of time to honor a victim.

The ordered lack of customary procedure during the Ron Brown plane crash investigation shows a desperate attempt to hide the facts. When you consider all of the following, this was clearly not what it was reported as:

- Ron Brown was being investigated for his involvement in Chinagate.

- Ron Brown was about to go public or talk to investigators.

- Hillary was the alleged mastermind behind Chinagate.

- Hillary was in Bosnia at the same airfield where Ron Brown's plane took off just before it crashed, only three days earlier.

- The Croatian government insisted on a Dubrovnik stop just 36 hours before Ron Brown's scheduled landing.

- The Air Force is told by the Clinton Administration to skip the initial investigation of why the plane crashed and just assume it was an accident.

- Enron executives take their own plane.

- Three days after the crash, a Croatian navigational engineer is found dead with a bullet in his chest. The death is ruled a suicide.

- X-rays of Ron Brown's head show a gunshot to the head.

- Pathologists who report the gunshot finding have a gag order placed on them.

- The Air Force cannot explain why the plane made a two-mile deviation into the mountains and crashed.

- Possible sabotage of the plane's electrical system.

- Possible Dubrovnik navigational system sabotage.

- The Clinton Administration did not tell the truth about the weather around Dubrovnik. They appeared to try and make it much worse than it was.

- President Clinton orders the cremation of all bodies.

- A passenger on the plane survives but on the way to the hospital dies due to a broken neck.

- Black boxes from the plane are recovered but then the Clinton Administration tells us there were no black boxes on that plane.

How many lies do you have to hear before you realize that something very, very creepy and devious is going on here? Ask yourself this: Who had the most to gain from the death of Ron Brown?

Chapter 13: Hillary Under Fire in Bosnia

In 1996, Hillary as First Lady, along with daughter Chelsea, made a trip to Bosnia. On more than one occasion, she embellishes her story stating they landed under sniper fire and had to run with their heads down for cover. News footage of the event shows she lied about the incident. It was rainy, and she appeared to keep her head down somewhat, but there was no sniper fire, and they didn't run for cover.

This is a perfect example of how a politician will say anything to elicit a desired response.

Almost ironically, this was only several days before Ron Brown would die on a plane that left that same airfield and would crash into a mountainside.

Some people are compulsive liars and can't stop. They exaggerate the truth to the extent that the majority calls it a lie. The filters of their brains work differently. It doesn't make it right; it's just a fact. When caught, they realize the mistake and cover it up as best they can with excuses like they can't remember, they made a mistake, or they make up another lie that they had never said it to begin with.

Chapter 14: Emailgate

In early 2015, a newspaper report revealed Secretary of State Hillary Clinton used her own private email server, rather than the one issued to her by the government. Investigations also reveal that the day of her first Senate hearing to become Secretary of State, Hillary Clinton or an associate purchased another private email server which was set up in her Chappaqua, New York, home. The incident gained widespread attention due to security concerns over possible hacking or surveillance.

Personal Server

In total, there were 62,320 emails at risk that Hillary Clinton had sent or received on the private email account in question. The separate server was allegedly set up as a matter of convenience so that she would only need to carry one device, not two. In retrospect, she admits it would have been better to have used a second email account and a second phone.

Questions remain as to whether Hillary Clinton signed Form OF-109, a standard document declaring she turned over all work-related records, upon her February 2013 resignation. After searching, the State Department stated it had no record that Hillary Clinton signed the form and was fairly certain she did not. In the research it was found that neither of her two immediate predecessors signed the forms. The form text warns individuals signing it that falsification is subject to criminal penalties under Section 1001 of Title 18. How convenient she didn't sign it.

Potential Mishandling of Classified Information

It was shown that the Inspectors General of the **Intelligence Community** and the **State Department** concluded there were hundreds of instances of classified information in the emails that originated from U.S. intelligence agencies, such as the **CIA** and the **NSA**.

Hillary can blame all the aides she wants as scapegoats, but the fact remains, she was in charge the whole time. It was all done under her direction. Having classified information on your private server is a "red flag."

It all began when the Intelligence Community Inspector General was brought in on a referral about Secretary Clinton's use of various personal email servers that she purchased during her time as Secretary of State. Also, various personal transmitting devices were used. The focus of the investigation was on whether any classified information was transmitted to or from her personal server system.

The investigation of approximately 30,000 emails at this point looked for evidence of classified information being improperly transmitted or stored on her personal email server. Emails and email chains were determined to be of a classified nature, some even Top Secret. Some emails that were not of a classified nature at the time have since been elevated and thus "up-classified" to where they are now confidential information.

Such an act of mishandling classified information, intentionally or by gross negligence, is a direct violation of a federal statute and is a felony. A second statute makes it a misdemeanor to knowingly remove classified information from such government systems or storage facilities.

Also investigated was whether there was evidence of computer hacking of the personal email server by any foreign entity or some other hostile group.

Additionally, interviews were conducted of everyone who could have been involved, such as technical people, staff, anyone who sent her emails, and Clinton herself.

Extensive work was done to look for signs of hacking. It was noted, no evidence of intentional deletion to conceal, misconduct, or hacking was found, but it was possible information was hacked.'

No case of criminal or willful mishandling or misconduct was found, and no charges were brought on Hillary Clinton. However, FBI Director Comey did strongly reprimand her for breaking the rules and that she should have known better. For her to get off with only a stern lecture shows the power associated through decades of political involvement, making connections with the right people which have apparently paid off. He also applied a double standard that someone else in this same situation would face charges, which makes no sense. Republicans as well as U.S. citizens in general were very upset at all of this, especially in view of the elections.

The problem with this is that her professional business is to be a trusted government employee whose primary goal is to make decisions to help keep this country secure. Hillary breached that trust by using a personal server. FBI investigations have uncovered many emails of a classified nature, and now we are finding some have even been up-classified to Top Secret, containing information sensitive to this nation's security.

Experts agree that the ramifications are huge and that in time they will become more apparent as the information that was hacked gets used against us.

If Hillary can't properly manage a tool as simple as email, how can she manage the job of president, or at this point, any other political office? The answer is she can't. Her flat answers reek of scandal and conspiracy.

The bottom line is that she should have known better as the intelligent (Yale Law School grad) government veteran that she is, and all she has to say is, "I made a mistake."

How many people have been fired for making less of a mistake, like Democratic National Convention Chair Wasserman Schultz who just resigned over pressure from the email fall-out?

For Comey to add that the State Department shared fault in the matter, apparently for not finding this out by themselves, is logical but not realistic. Who in their right mind would look into Hillary Clinton's (of all people) email use? Especially with a track record of bad things that happened to people who did stand up.

Even Hillary's allegations of trying to keep her personal business personal looks like she is trying to hide something. Wouldn't a secured government server be the securest place to keep any information? It's obvious no one was looking at her government account, or they would have found nothing as it was all on the personal server. What does she have to hide anyway, more scandals?

An interesting angle is if Hillary lied about not knowing that the private email server was a mistake. Speculating it was done on purpose, was the motive to pass classified information done in order to gain power and money? There is more to it all than meets the eye. If this is how Hillary handles her current post, then how will she improve if she becomes president when there is more at stake. What we are seeing is just the tip of the iceberg.

Chapter 15: Travelgate

This was a scandal about how the Clintons decided to make changes when they first came to the White House. One of the changes they made was to fire the White House travel office staff in order to hire friends and relatives. Although some may consider this a noble gesture of putting family and friends first, it should be noted how unprofessionally this was done. None of the employees was given any notice, and they were fired on the spot after having worked in their positions for a good many years.

An investigation was made, and five employees were put on administrative leave initially, then given other jobs in government as a consolation.

The travel office stems from the days of Andrew Jackson and serves to this day as the office that books the transportation of the White House Press Corps.

When protests were made about the firing decisions, Hillary allegedly requested the FBI do an investigation on Billy Dale, the former head of the White House travel office, for embezzlement. Dale was later audited by the IRS, which found he was not guilty, a common thing to happen to anyone crossing the path of the Clintons. His position was allegedly taken over by a cousin of Bill Clinton.

As a result of Independent Counsel Robert Ray's investigation in 2000, it was found that Hillary made statements that were factually false.

It was not determined if she had done so intentionally. As any good lawyer knows, it is proving the intent to lie, mislead, or cover up that makes it a chargeable offense. Mere ignorance is only reprimanded.

Chapter 16: Benghazi

On Sept. 11, 2012, U.S. Ambassador J. Christopher Stevens, U.S. Foreign Service Information Management Officer Sean Smith, and CIA contractors, Tyrone Woods and Glen Doherty, were killed by Islamic militants who attacked the American diplomatic compound in Benghazi, Libya.

Delayed response time resulted in these deaths in which two separate attacks were made. In fact, Ambassador Stevens' diary notes his concern regarding the lack of security and the requests for help that went unanswered.

The first American troops arrived after it was all over. It was the first time since 1979 that an American ambassador had been killed.

It was during this time that Hillary Clinton was the Secretary of State. The political instability of the area was growing, and repeated requests were made for additional security. The alarming fact is that in the months leading up to the attacks, Hillary's State Department actually cut security in Libya despite the heated situation.

Hindsight is always 20/20, but it can clearly be seen that Hillary's lack of providing sufficient security is what led to the numerous requests made for additional security.

The Back Story

Islamic militants were brought in, along with many weapons, for the 2011 Libyan Civil War that killed the then-leader of that country, Muammar Gaddafi. Ambassador Stevens was the first liaison with the party leading the revolution.

The aftermath left the country unstable with many small attacks going on daily. Three days before the siege there were reports of deteriorating security in the area of the compound.

Controversy surrounds the event as the temporary compound did not meet normal security specifications.

The Islamic militants came in trucks with the logo Ansar al-Sharia, a group working with the local government to provide security. They were heavily armed with AK-47s, grenades, other assault weapons, and cans of diesel fuel.

At first, the U.S. claimed the attacks were in response to a controversial video titled "Innocence of Muslims." This was an anti-Muslim film serving to spark protests. The U.S. mistakenly claimed it was these protests that led to the Benghazi compound attack to avoid making the attack look like an act of terrorism. However, Libyans interviewed stated no such protests occurred. Hillary's focus has remained that the video caused all this to happen, which does nothing to answer for her Department's lack of timely response that may have saved Americans.

Hillary also sent an email to her daughter telling her that terrorists were responsible but then told Americans that the attack was due to the movie. But Hillary should not take all the blame for this. President Obama was up for re-election, and he wanted Americans to believe this was an attack from a spontaneous demonstration and not a terrorist attack.

The assault wasn't sophisticated, but it was obvious the attackers had trained together and had clear orders on how to proceed. It was evident they had excellent intelligence, knowing how to get to different access points in the ambassador's compound and how to cut off the security guards.

What did happen is Special-Ops-trained independent security forces on assignment caught wind of the cries for assistance and responded on their own from another location. Traveling from Tripoli to Benghazi, they provided support during the two attacks.

Emails confirm protective forces could have moved swiftly to Benghazi if given the green light to do so. Hillary Clinton maintains other State Department professionals under her were assigned to make the decisions regarding security requests.

Adding to the issues is the fact that it took the FBI over three weeks to get to the Benghazi consulate to find only "cold" evidence. This made it much more difficult to investigate, and it took a long time before suspects in the slaying were identified and arrested.

Hillary's lack of response to send security to aid Stevens and the other Americans is morally reprehensible. It is the duty of the Secretary of State to decide to either secure the permission of another country for U.S. military to enter, or simply enter without permission.

Allegedly, part of the delay in sending help was because the State Department wasted time trying to figure out if military or civilian clothes should be worn, and if the vehicles they use should have identifiable U.S. markings. The idea concerning diplomacy was part of what held up the response.

Connection to Email Controversy

A recently discovered hidden email chain revealed how only hours after the siege began, troops could have immediately gone to Benghazi. Even with the classified information redacted, it is obvious the military was waiting for the orders to proceed, but no such order came. The mere fact this email was withheld, and for so long, only underscores that this was a scandal.

Chapter 17: Clinton Accounting While at the State Department

Another scandal involves accounting, where the State Department under Hillary Clinton could not account for about six billion dollars' worth of contracts made during the previous six years. Why it took six years to look into this to begin with is still a mystery.

State Department Accounting Investigation

In 2014, the Office of the Inspector General made an investigation and audit with a report noting the Department's failure to properly maintain the contract files along with inadequate contract control which thereby created financial risk.

Request for Documents

Also, when the Associated Press (AP) requested that the State Department turn over documents via the Freedom of Information Act (FOIA), they were kindly told they were too busy to respond at that time, but would provide them as soon as possible.

As can be deduced, there seemed to be deliberate withholding of possible evidence—as well as an effort to run the clock out of time—containing information that would make Hillary look bad in her initial stages of running for president in 2016. In the past, information had been "lost" and then later "found." As any good lawyer knows, you need evidence to convict.

The Cash Cow – The Clinton Foundation

There was an ethics agreement formed at the beginning of Hillary's term in the State Department between the State Department, Bill, and the Clinton Foundation that disclosure of details of donations be made as a means of "checks and balances."

Donations from foreign governments poured in. Bill had proven himself to be a prolific public speaker and savvy in meeting with foreign leaders and telling them things to entice them into contributing to such a cause.

The result is the Clinton Foundation had failed to disclose donors as agreed. Again, we see Hillary involved in breaking the rules and helping herself and Bill to make more money.

Another questionable donation was for $500,000 from Algeria in 2010, for earthquake relief in Haiti. This should have received a special ethics review due to the fact that it was not included in the continuation provision. The donation was made at the same time lobbying efforts of the State Department were undertaken by Algeria regarding their human rights record. In essence it was a payoff so as not to receive an unfavorable grade by Hillary's department on such a sensitive issue.

An analysis of records shows the State Department approved of almost all of Bill Clinton's speaking engagements although they lacked information about the value and links between them and possible donations. This shows Bill had carte blanche to make money any way he could for the Clinton Foundation with no obstacles. Also, the Clintons do not seem concerned about such things as pesky record keeping, as has been shown in the past.

During the period of 2009 through 2013, Rosatom, a Russian atomic energy agency, acquired Canadian uranium mining company Uranium One. This acquisition is interesting as Uranium One has rights to one-fifth of uranium mined in the U.S. Particularly sensitive is the fact this now goes to Russia. For the acquisition to be approved there had to be agreement between the Canadian government and a number of U.S. governmental bodies, one of which was the State Department. During the acquisition, Uranium One's chairman's family foundation conveniently made a multi-million-dollar donation to the Clinton Foundation. Bill Clinton also received a $500,000 payment from a Russian investment bank for making a speech in Moscow. Despite the ethics agreement, the donations were not disclosed by the Clinton Foundation or the State Department. As sneaky as it may have been, in this case, the donations going through the Canadian affiliate absolved the ethics agreement made. Although questions were raised there was no evidence of influence by Hillary in her official role. And let's not forget the illegal tax write-offs from the losses.

Chapter 18: Hillary on Women's Rights

Republicans, like Carly Fiorina, argue that it is hypocritical for Hillary Clinton to present herself as a champion of women's rights while the Clinton Foundation accepts major donations from countries like Saudi Arabia who do not have a very good record in their treatment of women.

Another knock on her is the lack of accomplishment on her resume toward supporting women. So far, all she has done is talk on the subject, but, talk is something. Words spoken and written are the tools used by diplomats, presidents, and journalists.

Still, whether she talked enough, forcefully and when it mattered, is a fair question. There is not much talk when it comes to the masses of women who risk coming forth with allegations against her husband, Bill.

She stood by Bill and he was a womanizer and she did nothing about that in defense of women. By sticking by him, she seems to condone his actions treating women with little or no respect. In fact, when it comes to her private life, she is not all that aggressive in her defense of women, as evidenced by what she said of Monica Lewinsky as a "narcissistic loony toon."

There is also the case of her 1975 defense of a 41-year-old man who allegedly raped a 12-year-old girl. Her tone on the audio interview is that she had a job to do and did it. All the evidence backed her client, whom she did not choose to defend. It was apparently her good lawyering that served to get a criminal off the hook.

In her favor, there is a report Hillary Clinton had ignored security concerns to visit refugees and survivors of sexual assault in the Democratic Republic of Congo back in 2009.

Friends and aides say while Hillary Clinton was on vacation that summer she sent many emails—albeit from her personal account—to get the department focused on the matter. Then, she dispatched some of her aides to determine what, if anything, could be done to make it more difficult for warlords to use the tactics of assault as a weapon of war and to warn camps of imminent invasions should they persist in using these tactics.

The efforts fell short mainly due to legal hurdles and from the non-cooperation of the Congolese government. But, Hillary Clinton's personal anguish and involvement convinced them that protecting women from violence was very important to her.

To her credit, Hillary Clinton was behind the adoption of a U.N. resolution that laid out guidelines for international response when sexual assault was discovered in war-torn areas.

During her speech at the Fourth World Conference on Women in Beijing in 1995, she fiercely argued how it was not acceptable to discuss women's rights as separate from human rights.

As is typical to Hillary's mindset, she took a calculated risk in each case, and had a specific, achievable goal in mind.

Chapter 19: Hillary for President

Superdelegates

Established in 1984, a superdelegate is basically a current or former democratic politician to the Democratic National Convention who is seated automatically and can support any candidate for the presidential nomination, and even switch sides. To have their vote count, they must attend and vote at the convention. The candidate with the most superdelegates has historically been a reliable indicator of who becomes the nominee.

Although they don't necessarily reflect the will of the people in their state, it does help to consider the opinion of those who elected them.

Back in 2008, Hillary Clinton led Obama by about 100 superdelegates, but that advantage shrank after Obama held a sustained advantage of pledged delegates. And in the end it was Obama who overtook her in superdelegates by the end of the primary season.

By the Numbers

Superdelegates make up 15 percent of all delegates, currently 714 out of 4,765, and are believed to be the path to winning the Democratic nomination. Superdelegates have never changed the outcome of the primary season.

The essence of this system in this election shows Hillary Clinton had a 15% head start over Sanders, which has him and others crying "foul." Obviously, during Hillary Clinton's time in politics she has built relationships with the right insiders who help influence this type of advantage.

Arguments are that this is what is, and has been, wrong with Washington—too many systems in place that end up keeping things as they are, as party roots run deep. Also, a candidate's electability by the rest of the country is an important factor the superdelegate keeps in mind.

Just another way Hillary uses her influence to get what she wants.

Chapter 20: Email Controversy Aftermath

Apparently, **22 million files of individuals** who applied for security clearances were stolen by Red China. These files contain in-depth electronic questionnaires (called EQIPs or EPSQs) from the applicants. Personal information such as marital status, criminal background, drug use/abuse, and more complete the file. Obviously, the loss of this critical information is devastating. In the wrong hands it can be used to blackmail a cleared individual, thus compromising security greatly.

The OPM Hack

The Office of Personnel Management (OPM) was hacked into, allegedly a result of Hillary Clinton's personal email server at her New York home.

The seriousness is such that the CIA pulled its agents out of Beijing for safety reasons. Also at risk are current and future military operations. It is predicted the compromised position we are now in could soon be revealed in tragic attacks.

The scope of risk is far-reaching, as it is believed many foreign intelligence agencies from other countries, including Russia, have also collected a virtual treasure trove of sensitive information vital to our national security.

In fact, as far back as 2011, Hillary's Chief of Staff, Cheryl Mills, warned her of the danger of using a personal email server. It is now coming to light that everyone involved with Hillary who was aware of the use of the personal server usage knew it was a violation and how it endangered national security.

New reports state there were an estimated 400 classified email messages on Hillary's personal server, with each carrying a felony violation subject to imprisonment of up to ten years.

Interestingly enough, a democratic operative admitted knowing Hillary used her personal server to avoid scrutiny of her shameful backroom activities.

The FBI investigated whether Hillary or her aides mishandled classified information intentionally or with gross negligence.

As no charges were brought against her, Hillary continues on with her run for president, however the resulting embarrassment is inevitable. Additionally, FBI Director Comey's lecture of Hillary's misconduct gives her opponents another opportunity to criticize her character, honesty, and trustworthiness which have been shown to be her biggest vulnerabilities. However, it seems Comey is still favoring Hillary, since he helped convict a Navy Reservist of mishandling classified materials. Bryan H. Nishimura pleaded guilty to unauthorized removal and retention of classified materials after the FBI found classified information stored in an unauthorized and unclassified system.

Hillary Clinton has numerous classified and top secret documents stored in an unauthorized location. What she did was on a larger scale then what Nishimura did, yet Hillary is not charged. In July of 2015, Nishimura was sentenced to two years of probation and a $7,500 fine. He was also required to surrender all government security clearances. Hillary Clinton has been given security briefings and could soon have the highest security clearance level if elected president. Why is it always that the little guy pays the full price, but Hillary pays no price?

Hillary's constant reiteration through all this is she made a mistake and won't do it again.

Trump rightfully tweeted that adversaries of the U.S. most certainly have a file which they can utilize to possibly blackmail her and this fact alone should now disqualify Hillary from even running for president. He added that the verdict of no charges handed down by the FBI is damning evidence the current political system is rigged, and pointed to Bill's meeting with Lynch in her private plane.

The resulting overall consensus is that Hillary is above the law. The damage done is a terrible precedent that has been set leaving a sour taste in the mouths of U.S. citizens.

A request has been made to the Director of National Intelligence to block Hillary's access to further classified information.

Republican National Committee Chairman Reince Priebus is beside himself regarding the FBI's decision, and deservedly so, stating the clear and gross negligence Hillary demonstrated should have resulted in charges, adding that Hillary Clinton had lied.

The House Select Committee investigation uncovered Hillary's admission that she used her private email server on Benghazi. Theorists believe this may have led to the siege there that killed the four Americans.

She said it was a mistake and that she regrets doing it and would not do that again.

Republican National Convention spokesman Michael Short made a statement that he feels Hillary Clinton is withholding the truth and broke the rules regarding her email server, compromising national security in the process. The only things made clear is her intent to mislead voters by obscuring the facts and her reckless conduct while secretary of state.

The State Department focus has now shifted to whether current employees who were involved in the handling, sending, and receiving of 'Hillary's emails should receive some form of disciplinary action. This could range from a reprimand to the total loss of their security clearance. Former employees found guilty of mishandling classified information could have notes put in their permanent file that could draw consequences should they seek government employment in the future that would require a security clearance.

House Oversight Committee Chairman Jason Chaffetz stated he will request an FBI probe into whether or not Hillary Clinton lied about her email server to Congress as the consensus is she failed in her role as secretary of state to follow the rules and inform key departmental staff of her actions regarding the use of her private email server.

Chapter 21: Enter Attorney General Loretta Lynch

The fact is Bill Clinton met with Attorney General Loretta Lynch privately in her jet. Speculation was made he was pleading for Hillary and the email controversy, but there were no witnesses as to what was actually discussed. This meeting was said to be a chance meeting. This is highly unlikely since Loretta and her husband were waiting in their jet for Bill Clinton's plane to land. The meeting was set up to be a secret. The cover story that Clinton and Lynch made up was that they just talked about family.

It must be taken into consideration that Bill appointed Lynch as U.S. Attorney for the Eastern District of New York in 1999—a powerful position overseeing Wall Street and handling cases on some of the most wealthy and influential people in the country.

It was possible Bill Clinton was also pleading for himself as he is an official person of interest in a number of investigations by the Department of Justice. In any event, the meeting was a violation of the Justice Department's policy on communicating with a side in a case, and the rules of impartiality may have been compromised.

There is also the possibility that Bill Clinton was making a deal such that if Attorney General Loretta Lynch did not bring any charges against Hillary Clinton then Hillary Clinton would keep Loretta Lynch as the Attorney General of the United States.

Judical Watch, a conservative organization, has stated "Attorney General Lynch's decision to breach the well-defined ethical standards of the Department of Justice and the American legal pofession is an outrageous abuse of the public's trust." Judicial Watch on June 30, 2016, requested that the U.S. Department of Justice Office of the Inspector General investigate the meeting between Bill Clinton and Attorney General Loretta Lynch.

Chapter 22: The Clinton Foundation

The Clinton Foundation is a non-profit corporation under section 501 of the United States tax code. It was founded by Bill Clinton with the mission statement being to "strengthen the capacity of people in the United States and throughout the world to meet the challenges of global interdependence." The website of the organization is clintonfoundation.org. As of September 11, 2016, the website's FAQ page states, "The Bill, Hillary & Chelsea Clinton Foundation builds partnerships between businesses, NGOs, governments, and individuals everywhere to work faster, better, and leaner; to find solutions that last; and to transform lives and communities from what they are today to what they can be tomorrow."

Bill Clinton currently serves as President, and Chelsea Clinton, the daughter of Bill and Hillary, serves as Vice Chair of the Board. The Board is also stacked with former and current Bill and Hillary associates such as Bruce Lindsey and Cheryl Mills, a lawyer and aid to Hillary Clinton.

The Clinton Foundation website states that the foundation helps more than 31,000 American schools with healthy food choices in an effort to eradicate childhood obesity. The website also states that they provide climate-smart agronomic training for higher farmer crop yields in Malawi, Rwanda, and Tanzania.

The Foundation website also states that each year they have reduced 33,500 tons of greenhouse gas emissions in the United States. They state that they are helping with social enterprises in Latin America, the Caribbean, and Asia. They provide people all over the world with CHAI-negotiated prices for HIV/AIDS medications.

In 2014, according to the Clinton Foundation's consolidated statement of financial position, the Foundation took in $112 million in contributions. This is more than double what they reported in 2013. Where did this increase in funding come from? It turns out that much of the money has been raised from foreign individuals.

The New York Times stated the serious nature of having Hillary Clinton run for president of the United States while her husband is raising millions of dollars from foreign individuals. *The Washington Post*'s columnist David Ignatius also found this practice outrageous. He went on to say that wealthy foreign individuals could influence the United States.

MSNBC's Morning Joe reported on Hillary running for president and Bill Clinton collecting funds for the Foundation as "It's just wrong."

Bradley A. Blakeman in a Newsmax.com atricle wrote, "It is clear that there exists probable cause to believe both Hillary and Bill Clinton used a public office (secretary of state and a charity, the Clinton Foundation) in a pay to play scheme of criminal conduct and conspiracy with the aim to provide access and favors from government officials, including but not limited to, the secretary of state in exchange for donations made to the Clinton Foundation, as well as direct payments to Bill Clinton as speaking and consulting fees by individuals (foreign and domestic as well as foreign government officials and states)."

Bernie Sanders, the former democratic challenger to Hillary Clinton has stated on NBC's *Meet the Press* that Hillary Clinton "should cease all operations, all contact" with the Clinton Foundation if she wins the presidency.

Hillary clearly does not see the issue of Bill Clinton being President of the Foundation while she is president. On September 5, 2016, Hillary Clinton was asked about her husband's role in the Clinton Foundation. Here is what she said: "I don't think there are conflicts of interest," she said in the interview. "I know that that's what has been alleged and never proven. But nevertheless, I take it seriously."

In the same interview Hillary Clinton also stated, "I feel very good about my service as secretary of state. No decision I ever made was influenced by anybody. What I made a decision based on was what was good for the United States, what was good for our values, our interests, and our security. And the State Department has confirmed there's no evidence of any such influence at all."

What is especially troubling about this is if Hillary Clinton believes there is nothing wrong with this now, then clearly a president Clinton would see no issue with funneling billions of dollars wherever she wants. Who would stop her? She would have Loretta Lynch, an already compromised individual caught in the Clinton web as the Attorney General. The congress would be powerless to do anything. They could impeach Hillary in the same way that Bill Clinton was impeached. But the Senate would never convict her. It would simply be labeled a partisan witch hunt and no democrat would vote to convict her. The Obama Administration has seen nothing wrong with sending 400 million dollars in CASH to IRAN which just by pure chance happened on the same day that Iran released captive Americans according to President Barak Obama. With the U.S. government dealing in cash to allegedly work around banking laws that the United States helped set up, one can only imagine what Hillary Clinton would do. There seems to be a clear ethics problem with Hillary's thinking.

In August of 2016, a new batch of emails shows that the U.S. State Department gave special access to a Clinton Foundation donor, Claudio Osorio, while Hillary was Secretary of State. Mr. Osorio received $10 million from the government after the Clinton State Department facilitated the deal from the Overseas Investment Corporation (OPIC) which is a federal agency that operates under the State Department. Mr. Osorio's project was to build houses in Haiti after the 2010 earthquake. The project never broke ground and Osorio used the money to support his millionaire-like lifestyle. Federal prosecutors said that Osorio was sentenced and sent to prison in 2013. The big story here is that a Clinton Foundation donor was given access, which allowed him to secure $10 million for a sham project. Transactions like this make it hard to believe Hillary Clinton when she says, "there's no evidence of any such influence at all."

Bill has been working in the background helping support Hillary's campaign and to build Clinton wealth, by lecturing, writing, and using his influence to get secret donations from sheiks, tycoons, and magnates from around the world. The number and amount of donations quite possibly violates the Memorandum of Understanding (MOU) that limits foreign donations. The Memorandum was an agreement between the Clinton Foundation and the United States government. The memorandum was to limit foreign contributions from foreign governments that wanted to influence the policy of the United States. What is shocking is that if you look at the donors to the Clinton Foundation there are numerous donations from foreign governments.

The Clinton Foundation and the Clinton Health Access Initiative have both ignored New York laws requiring them to disclose the names of foreign donors. The New York State Attorney General has not attempted to enforce the law. The fact that money is coming into these Clinton organizations from undisclosed foreign individuals hides who could be trying to influence the United States. That said, the Clinton Foundation does list the source of the money, even if they don't name an individual. In many cases it is a corporation, a foundation, or a foreign government. Below is a list of Foundation donors that contributed more than $250,000 since the Foundation was started until the second quarter of 2016.

Greater than $25,000,000

Bill & Melinda Gates Foundation
Clinton Giustra Enterprise Partnership (Canada) *
Fred Eychaner and Alphawood Foundation
Frank Giustra, The Radcliffe Foundation
Nationale Postcode Loterij
The Children's Investment Fund Foundation
UNITAID

$10,000,000 to $25,000,000

AUSAID **
Stephen L. Bing
Commonwealth of Australia ** *
COPRESIDA

Tom Golisano ^
J.B. and M.K. Pritzker Family Foundation *
Kingdom of Norway [Government of Norway] **
Kingdom of Saudi Arabia
Denis J. O'Brien and Digicel *
Cheryl and Haim Saban & The Saban Family Foundation
Susie Tompkins Buell Fund of the Marin Community Foundation
The Elma Foundation
The Hunter Foundation *
The Rockefeller Foundation
The Swedish Postcode Lottery
The Victor Pinchuk Foundation
Theodore W. Waitt

$5,000,001 to $10,000,000
S. Daniel Abraham
Sheikh Mohammed H. Al-Amoudi
C40 Cities Climate Leadership Group, Inc.
Elton John Aids Foundation
Government of the Netherlands **
Irish Aid **
John D. Mackay
Norwegian Agency for Development Cooperation (NORAD) **
OCP Corporation
Michael Schumacher
State of Kuwait
The Clinton Family Foundation
The Coca-Cola Company *
The Wasserman Foundation
Tracfone Wireless, Inc.

$1,000,001 to $5,000,000
100 Women in Hedgefunds
Absolute Return for Kids (ARK)
Acxiom Corporation
Jay Alix
Alliance for a Green Revolution in Africa
Nasser Al-Rashid

American Federation of Teachers *
Angelopoulos Foundation ^
Gianna Angelopoulos ^
Anheuser-Busch Foundation
Smith and Elizabeth Bagley
Banc of California ^ *
Barclays Capital ^
Barclays plc
Mary Bing and Doug Ellis
Bloomberg Philanthropies
Blue Cross and Blue Shield of North Carolina ^
Richard Blum and Blum Family Foundation
BMU - Federal Ministry for the Environment **
Booz Allen Hamilton ^
Carlos Bremer
Richard Caring
Gilbert R. Chagoury
Cheniere Energy, Inc.
Christy and John Mack Foundation
Cisco ^ *
Gustavo Cisneros & Venevision *
Citi Foundation ^
Clinton-Bush Haiti Fund
Stephen J. Cloobeck
Roy E. Cockrum
Victor P. Dahdaleh & The Victor Phillip Dahdaleh
Charitable Foundation
Delos Living ^
Desert Classic Charities Inc
Robert Disbrow
Dubai Foundation
Duke Energy Corporation ^ *
EKTA Foundation
Entergy
Exxonmobil ^
Issam M. Fares
Raj Fernando
Ferraro Family Foundation
Fidelity Charitable Gift Fund
Joseph T. Ford
Wallace W. Fowler

Friends Of Saudi Arabia
Fundacion Telmex
Mala Gaonkar Haarman
GEMS Education

$500,001 to $1,000,000

Abraaj Holdings ^
Akwa Group ^
Alibaba Group
Malini Alles
amfAR: The Foundation for AIDS Research
Andrade Gutierrez S.A. ^
Arizona State University ^
Arkansas Economic Development Commission [Arkansas Energy Office - Arkansas Economic Development] **
Atlas Group Limited
William and Tani Austin
Autodesk, Inc. *
Bank of America Foundation
Simón P. Barceló
Barlovento Foundation
Frederick Baron and Lisa Blue
Laurie and Bill Benenson
Arpad Busson
Alonzo Cantu
John and Margo Catsimatidis
Chevron Corporation ^
Citigroup Inc *
Confederaç?o Nacional da Indústria (CNI) ^
Confédération Générale des Entreprises du Maroc (CGEM) ^
Confederation of Indian Industry ^
Michael J. Cooper
Crabby Beach Foundation
Lewis B. Cullman
Daimler Trucks North America LLC
Dell Inc.
Depart of Finance & Admin. - State Fiscal Stabilization Fund **
Dozoretz Family Foundation

Emerson Collective *
Energy Developments and Investments Corporation ^
Foreign Affairs, Trade and Development Canada (DFATD) **

Fundación Carlos Slim
Matias Garfunkel ^
Gill Foundation
Avram A. and Jill H. Glazer Family
Global Impact *
Jane Goldman
Rolando González Bunster *
Google Inc. *
Brian L. Greenspun
Grupo ABC ^
Hernreich Family Foundation *
Patricia A. Hotung
InterEnergy
Jill and Ken Iscol
Itaú Unibanco S/A ^
J/P Haitian Relief Organization

$250,001 to $500,000

Billye and Henry Aaron *
Accoona Corporation
Abbas I. Al Yousef
Altman/Kazickas Foundation
American Association of University Women ^
American Federation of State, County and Municipal Employees
American International Group, Inc. (AIG) ^
American University in Dubai
Amil Assistlncia Médica Internacional S/A ^
Anim LLC
AstraZeneca Pharmaceuticals LP
James A. Attwood
Farhad Azima
Fred Bacher
Banco Santander Brasil S.A. ^
Barrick Gold Corporation
Anson and Debra Beard

Jack C. Bendheim
BMCE Bank ^
Oliver Bock
Bill Brandt, Patrice Bugelas-Brandt, and Development Specialists, Inc.
 [Development Specialists, Inc.]
Bright Future International
Susie and Mark Buell
CA Technologies ^ *
Paul L. Cejas
Centene Charitable Foundation
CH2M ^
Channel IT ^
Charles Dunstone Charitable Trust
Charles Stewart Mott Foundation *
City of Little Rock **
Compania De Electricidad De San Pedro De Macoris (Cespm)
Consolidated Contractors Inter. Co. Sal ^
Crédit Agricole du Maroc [Groupe Credit Agricole du Maroc] ^
Beverly Dale *
Martin Davis
Oscar de la Renta
Deutsche Bank AG ^
Deutsche Bank Americas ^
Yongping Duan
Nancy Ellison and William Rollnick
Niko Elmaleh
Embassy of Algeria
Jana and Richard Fant
Morad N. Fareed
Fisher Brothers Foundation, Inc.
Freeport-McMoRan Copper & Gold Foundation ^
Freeport-McMoRan Inc. ^ *
Fuel Freedom Foundation ^
J. B. Fuqua

$250,001 to $500,000
Billye and Henry Aaron *

Accoona Corporation
Abbas I. Al Yousef
Altman/Kazickas Foundation
American Association of University Women ^
American Federation of State, County and Municipal Employees
American International Group, Inc. (AIG) ^
American University in Dubai
Amil Assistîncia Médica Internacional S/A ^
Anim LLC
AstraZeneca Pharmaceuticals LP
James A. Attwood
Farhad Azima
Fred Bacher
Banco Santander Brasil S.A. ^
Barrick Gold Corporation
Anson and Debra Beard
Jack C. Bendheim
BMCE Bank ^
Oliver Bock
Bill Brandt, Patrice Bugelas-Brandt, and Development Specialists, Inc. [Development Specialists, Inc.]
Bright Future International
Susie and Mark Buell
CA Technologies ^ *
Paul L. Cejas
Centene Charitable Foundation
CH2M ^
Channel IT ^
Charles Dunstone Charitable Trust
Charles Stewart Mott Foundation *
City of Little Rock **
Compania De Electricidad De San Pedro De Macoris (Cespm)
Consolidated Contractors Inter. Co. Sal ^
Crédit Agricole du Maroc [Groupe Credit Agricole du Maroc] ^
Beverly Dale *
Martin Davis
Oscar de la Renta
Deutsche Bank AG ^Deutsche Bank Americas ^

Yongping Duan
Nancy Ellison and William Rollnick
Niko Elmaleh
Embassy of Algeria
Jana and Richard Fant
Morad N. Fareed
Fisher Brothers Foundation, Inc.
Freeport-McMoRan Copper & Gold Foundation ^
Freeport-McMoRan Inc. ^ *
Fuel Freedom Foundation ^
J. B. Fuqua

^ Indicates contributions exclusively for CGI activities such as memberships, sponsorships, and conference fees.
* Indicates a contribution was made by this donor in the second quarter of 2016.
** Indicates government grants.

Chapter 23: Putting It All Together

As anyone can plainly see, there are resounding similarities, patterns if you will, between all these scandals that have happened over the last 38 years, which only means two things: Hillary is a compulsive liar only out for her best, self-serving interests, and that she will never stop.

Democratic Presidential Nominee

The next item on her agenda is to be president. Amid the clouds of scandal on her horizon, each move she makes in her career involves higher stakes with regard to power and money. Even if she doesn't win, she will still have made a lot of money in the campaign process.

Just as a leopard cannot change its spots, Hillary has not, cannot, and will not change. She continues to lie and break the rules to maintain her position or get ahead. In the end it's always the same old story.

Regarding her achievements, Hillary's only miraculous accomplishment has been staying out of jail. She has been embroiled in so many investigations through the years that have clearly shown her to be in the wrong, but due to missing evidence or the death of someone who was to testify, has never been charged.

Political pundits are in agreement as to her shortcomings from all the fiascoes over the years and how all of this is negatively impacting her ratings at this crucial time before the fall elections take place.

Hillary Clinton has repeatedly threatened the security of this country by using her personal email server to send and receive classified emails. With regard to the Rose Law Firm billing records case in which records went missing then copies were found, how would that work if she were to become president? A point to be made is that after the files and records go "missing," they somehow then get "found" once Hillary and Bill are cleared.

Obviously her history shows beyond the preponderance of a doubt that there will be more things of greater severity as she seems to be getting more brazen with age.

How can we make decisions based on lies? Lying in a court of law is a crime and punishable. And here we have a lawyer running for the highest office in the land who has repeatedly lied to the country for decades in every position she has held, yet has still been allowed to continue on because of cover-ups, favors called in, and backroom deals.

Choosing Her VP

As far as her Vice President pick of Tim Kaine goes, he really can't help her look honest, and no one votes just for the bottom half of the ticket. She needs him like she needed Bill. He is everything she is not and together they complement each other. They both share the will to fight for progressive causes.

Fall Elections

Before you vote, which I hope you will, take a while to think about the facts, not just the hype and static propaganda generated by the heat of the debates. Ask yourself the proven, strategic questions:

- Has Hillary shown honest consistency putting the needs of the masses before her own throughout her career?

- Who do you trust the most from what they accomplished, not what they said?

- Did you ever trust a person after you found out they lied or deceived you?

- Realize that there are more than two political parties. If you don't like the person running in the Democratic Party, this does not mean that you need to vote for the Republican Party. You can vote for the Libertarian Party, or even the Green Party.

The answers may help to enable you to make a decision you can live with for at least four years.

Armed with this information, many people don't believe Hillary Clinton is fit to be president as demonstrated by her dwindling popularity ratings. With Hillary there is always someone to blame, even if it's her own ignorance. We need capable leaders in these mediocre times. A vote for her is a vote for scandal.

If Hillary Clinton is voted in with her record for the world to see, what will this say about our nation to foreign countries? Are we ready for President Hillary Clinton and First Gentleman Bill? The nations of the world are watching this election closely. If she wins the election, watch out America, they may not view us as rational or intelligent as was once perceived.

Conclusion

I hope this book was able to help you get a better understanding of the vast number of scandals over many years that Hillary Clinton has been involved in, and the character of the person who is the democratic candidate running in this year's presidential election.

The next step is to approach this material with an open mind before asking yourself if this is the type of scandalous individual you want running our country. Four years can be a long time to wait for another election.

Finally, if you enjoyed this book, please take the time to share your thoughts and post a review on Amazon. It would be greatly appreciated!

Thank you and good luck!

References:

Watergate, Whitewater, Vince Foster, Cattle Futures, Use of IRS, Chinagate, Lying about Bosnia, Hillary & Women's Rights:
http://www.wnd.com/2015/05/here-they-are-hillarys-22-biggest-scandals-ever/

https://en.wikipedia.org/wiki/Hillary_Rodham_cattle_futures_controversy
http://community.seattletimes.nwsource.com/archive/?date=19940330&slug=1902853

Vince Foster Information:
http://www.dailymail.co.uk/news/article-508210/The-man-knew-The-truth-death-Hillary-Clintons-close-friend-Vince-Foster.html
http://www.wnd.com/2015/05/here-they-are-hillarys-22-biggest-scandals-ever/#!

http://www.thepoliticalinsider.com/new-documents-prove-hillary-clinton-murder-cover/
https://whatyouthoughtiwentaway.wordpress.com/2016/03/02/the-resignation-letter-of-vince-foster/

http://www.wnd.com/2016/02/vince-foster-suicide-shocker-2nd-wound-documented/#!
http://www.liberalforum.org/index.php?/topic/188228-breaking-story-vince-fosters-2nd-wound/

Bill Clinton Indiscretions:
https://en.wikipedia.org/wiki/Bill_Clinton_sexual_misconduct_allegations

http://www.albertpeia.com/oxfordassault.htm
https://www.washingtonpost.com/news/post-politics/wp/2016/03/06/in-an-unusual-allusion-to-bill-clintons-sexual-affair-hillary-clinton-speaks-of-forgiveness/

http://www.refinery29.com/2014/07/71602/hillary-clinton-forgiving-bill-cheating
http://enquirer.com/editions/2003/06/09/tem_monlede09.html

Healthcare Reform 1993:
https://www.boundless.com/u-s-history/textbooks/boundless-u-s-history-textbook/bush-clinton-and-a-changing-world-31/the-clinton-administration-231/the-health-care-plan-of-1993-1317-9290/

Chinagate:
http://www.wnd.com/2015/05/here-they-are-hillarys-22-biggest-scandals-ever/

Ron Brown:
http://www.wnd.com/2013/04/ron-brown-was-hillarys-1st-chris-stevens/#!

http://www.wnd.com/2004/09/26786/#
http://dangerouslogic.com/ron_brown.html

http://www.whatreallyhappened.com/RANCHO /CRASH/BROWN/brown.php#axzz4Jy57i4yN

http://www.whatreallyhappened.com/RANCHO /CRASH/BROWN/bullet.html

Hillary as Secretary of State & Benghazi:
http://www.powerlineblog.com/archives/2016/ 06/is-hillary-to-blame-for-the-lack-of-a-military-response-in-benghazi.php

http://www.rawstory.com/2016/02/this-is-what-actually-happened-at-the-us-consulate-in-benghazi/

http://www.thepoliticalinsider.com/breaking-smoking-gun-docs-show-hillary-clinton-knew-benghazi-along-whoa/

http://www.judicialwatch.org/press-room/press-releases/judicial-watch-new-benghazi-email-shows-dod-offered-state-department-forces-that-could-move-to-benghazi-immediately-specifics-blacked-out-in-new-document/

Accounting in State Dept.:
https://en.wikipedia.org/wiki/Hillary_Clinton% 27s_tenure_as_Secretary_of_State

Women's Rights:
http://www.bloomberg.com/politics/articles/20 15-03-10/hillary-clinton-s-long-cautious-record-on-women-s-rights

Superdelegates:
http://www.msnbc.com/msnbc/how-do-superdelegates-work-heres-what-you-need-know

http://www.npr.org/2015/11/13/455812702/clinton-has-45-to-1-superdelegate-advantage-over-sanders

Email Server Scandal:
http://www.independentsentinel.com/attack-scenario-how-hillary-clintons-lust-for-money-and-power-led-to-americas-digital-pearl-harbor/

http://www.cnn.com/2016/07/07/politics/state-department-reopens-probe-into-clinton-emails/index.html

http://www.cnn.com/2016/07/05/politics/fbi-director-doesnt-recommend-charges-against-hillary-clinton/

https://www.fbi.gov/news/pressrel/press-releases/statement-by-fbi-director-james-b.-comey-on-the-investigation-of-secretary-hillary-clintons-use-of-a-personal-e-mail-system
http://www.judicialwatch.org/blog/2016/07/comeys-fbi-helped-convict-navy-reservist-handled-classified-materials-inappropriately/

Loretta Lynch:

http://www.trunews.com/article/did-bill-clinton-cut-a-plea-deal-with-lynch-for-hillary

Verdit, A News Publication from Judicial Watch, September, 2016, Vol. 22, Issue 9

Hillary Lying to Congress:
http://www.newsmax.com/Newsmax-Tv/dick-morris-hillary-clinton-fbi-email/2016/07/07/id/737655/

Foundation:
http://www.newsmax.com/Newsfront/David-Ignatius-Clinton-Foundation-Foreign-Donations-Wrong/2016/08/31/id/746106/

http://www.newsmax.com/BradleyBlakeman/email-foundation/2016/08/30/id/745915/

http://www.newsmax.com/Politics/Sanders-Hillary-Clinton-Foundation-Campaign/2016/09/04/id/746638/

http://www.newsmax.com/Politics/hillary-clinton-foundation-charity/2016/09/06/id/746996/

http://www.newsmax.com/newsfront/daily-caller-clinton-foundation-lied-irs/2016/09/08/id/747318/

http://msnbcmedia.msn.com/i/msnbc/sections/news/understanding.pdf

http://www.judicialwatch.org/blog/2016/08/hillary-state-dept-helped-jailed-clinton-foundation-donor-get-10-mil-u-s-failed-haiti-project/

www.ingramcontent.com/pod-product-compliance
Lightning Source LLC
Chambersburg PA
CBHW070159290526
45789CB00002B/841